The Wisdom of Words:
A Collection of Favorite Quotes

Sarah Khalil A.A

Title:

- Journal Of Life (2022)

Upcoming Books:

- The Haunted Queen
- Debut Book Series
"Unfinished Stories"
Book 1" The Hour Of Love

https://www.instagram.com/authorsarahkaa/

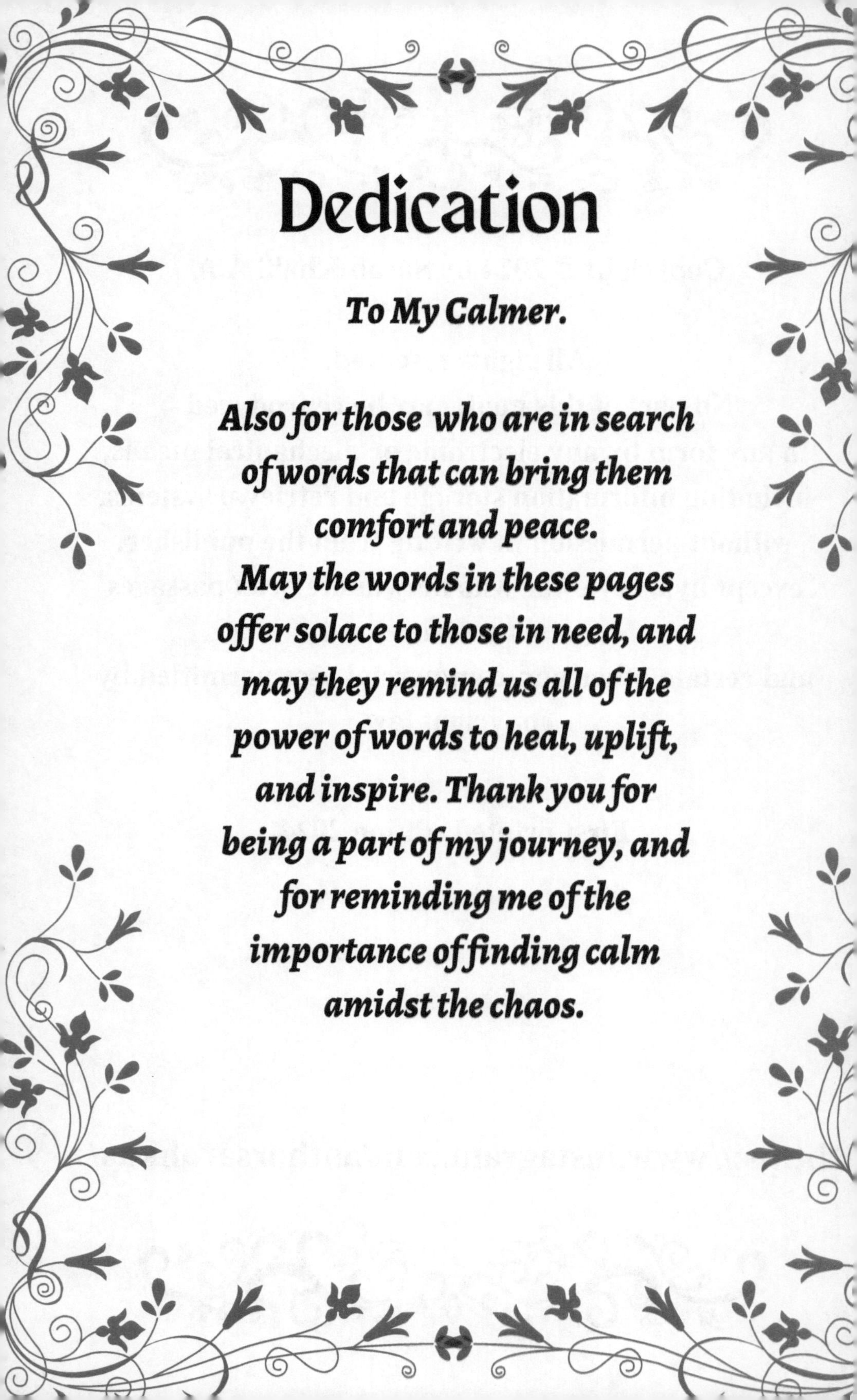

Dedication

To My Calmer.

Also for those who are in search of words that can bring them comfort and peace. May the words in these pages offer solace to those in need, and may they remind us all of the power of words to heal, uplift, and inspire. Thank you for being a part of my journey, and for reminding me of the importance of finding calm amidst the chaos.

Introduction:

Words are a powerful tool, capable of inspiring, motivating, comforting, and enlightening us. They have the ability to express our deepest emotions, convey complex ideas, and connect us with each other in meaningful ways. Throughout history, words have been used to inspire movements, shape cultures, and transform societies.

In "The Wisdom of Words: A Collection of Favorite Quotes," we have compiled a collection of some of the most profound and thought-provoking quotes from some of the greatest minds in history. From philosophers and writers to artists and scientists, these individuals have left an indelible mark on the world through their words. This book is not just a compilation of random quotes, but rather a carefully curated selection of insights and ideas that have stood the test of time. Each quote has been chosen for its ability to inspire, challenge, and uplift us. Whether you are looking for guidance in your personal life, seeking inspiration for a creative project, or simply looking for a thought-provoking read, "The Wisdom of Words" has something for you.

So, take a moment to immerse yourself in the wisdom of these great minds, and let their words inspire and guide you on your own journey.

To forgive is the highest , most beautiful form of love. In return, you will receive untold peace and happiness.

I no longer grieve while I believe in my lord, and if the pain over takes me, I remember the status of those who are patient.

3

"There were grief and ruins,
and you were the miracle"

-Pablo Neruda, "A Song of Despair"

"Books, she has found, are a way to live a thousand lives-- or to find strength in a very long one."

—V.E. Schwab, The Invisible Life of Addie LaRue

"And this, he decides, is what a good-bye should be.
Not a period, but an ellipsis, a statement trailing off until someone is there to pick it up.
It is a door left open.
It is drifting off to sleep"
— Invisible Life of Addie Larue
*recommended by @mia.read.it

6

"Courage is one thing that no one can ever take away from you."
— Chris Colfer, The Wishing Spell

"The world will always choose convenience over reality. It's easier to hate, blame, and fear than it is to understand. No one wants the truth; they want entertainment."
— Chris Colfer, The Wishing Spell

"The only thing we have
inside us is hope, hope that
pulls us from our miseries,
hopes
that keep us going and enable
us to carry on; a hope that one
day someone will hear our
voices and help spread our
message
to the world."
— Sarah Khalil A.A., Journal Of Life

> "Imperfection is beauty, madness is genius and it's better to be absolutely ridiculous than absolutely boring."
>
> — Marilyn Monroe

"Yesterday is history, tomorrow is a mystery, today is a gift of God, which is why we call it the present."
— Bill Keane

> "I have not failed. I've just found 10,000 ways that won't work."
>
> — Thomas A. Edison

"This life is what you make it. No matter what, you're going to mess up sometimes, it's a universal truth. But the good part is you get to decide how you're going to mess it up. Girls will be your friends - they'll act like it anyway. But just remember, some come, some go. The ones that stay with you through everything - they're your true best friends. Don't let go of them. Also remember, sisters make the best friends in the world. As for lovers, well, they'll come and go too. And baby, I hate to say it, most of them - actually pretty much all of them are going to break your heart, but you can't give up because if you give up, you'll never find your soulmate. You'll never find that half who makes you whole and that goes for everything. Just because you fail once, doesn't mean you're gonna fail at everything. Keep trying, hold on, and always, always, always believe in yourself, because if you don't, then who will, sweetie? So keep your head high, keep your chin up, and most importantly, keep smiling, because life's a beautiful thing and there's so much to smile about."
— Marilyn Monroe

13

"And, when you want something, all the universe conspires in helping you to achieve it."

— Paulo Coelho, The Alchemist

"How beautiful of you to smile at times when your heart wants to cry"

15

"The world will always choose convenience over reality. It's easier to hate, blame, and fear than it is to understand. No one wants the truth; they want entertainment."
— Chris Colfer, The Wishing Spell

"When we love, we always strive to become better than we are. When we strive to become better than we are, everything around us becomes better too."

— Paulo Coelho, The Alchemist

"I hope no one who reads this book has been quite as miserable as Susan and Lucy were that night; but if you have been - if you've been up all night and cried till you have no more tears left in you - you will know that there comes in the end a sort of quietness. You feel as if nothing is ever going to happen again."

— C.S. Lewis, The Lion, the Witch and the Wardrobe

"I wrote this story for you, but when I began it I had not realized that girls grow quicker than books. As a result you are already too old for fairy tales, and by the time it is printed and bound you will be older still. But some day you will be old enough to start reading fairy tales again. You can then take it down from some upper shelf, dust it, and tell me what you think of it. I shall probably be too deaf to hear, and too old to understand a word you say, but I shall still be your affectionate Godfather, C. S. Lewis."
— C.S. Lewis, The Lion, the Witch and the Wardrobe

"One of the most cowardly things ordinary people do is to shut their eyes to facts."
—C.S. Lewis, Chronicles of Narnia: The Voyage of the Dawn Treader

"The will to be polite, to maintain civility and normalcy, is fearfully strong. I wonder sometimes how much evil is permitted to run unchecked simply because it would be rude to interrupt it."
- Alix E Harrow in Ten Thousand Doors of January
*recommended by @moonlitbookmoth

"If I read a book and it makes my whole body so cold no fire can warm me, I know that is poetry. If I feel physically as if the top of my head were taken off, I know that is poetry. These are the only ways I know it. Is there any other way?"
— Emily Dickinson
*recommended by @bookandteabook

"Those who have knowledge and do
not share it, resemble the dead."
— Aisha (RA)

*recommended by @bookish_katastrophe

'Every atom of me and every atom of you...We'll live in birds and flowers and dragonflies and pine trees and in clouds and in those little specks of light you see floating in sunbeams...And when they use our atoms to make new lives, they won't just be able to take one, they'll have to take two, one of you and one of me, we'll be joined so tight..."
— The Amber Spyglass - Philip Pullman
*recommended by @every.atom.reads

"It does not do to dwell on dreams and forget to live."

—J.K. Rowling, Harry Potter and the Sorcerer's Stone

"The world will always choose convenience over reality. It's easier to hate, blame, and fear than it is to understand. No one wants the truth; they want entertainment."
— Chris Colfer, The Wishing Spell

"distance is not for the fearful, it's for the bold. It's for those who are willing to spend a lot of time alone in exchange for a little time with the one they love. It's for those who know a good thing when they see it, even if they don't see it nearly enough"

*recommended by @shiros.world

"Once we figure out what we are good at, that's our cue to bulldoze through, master the skill and keep pushing, till we reach the top of the pyramid."

— Rida khan

*recommended by @bookish_katastrophe

28

"The world is a book, and those who do not travel read only a page."
— Saint Augustine
*recommended by @mamarachauthor

"I have lived a thousand lives and I've loved a thousand loves. I've walked on distant worlds and seen the end of time. Because I read."

— George R.R. Martin, *A Dance with Dragons*

*recommended by @mamarachauthor

"No matter how much you love someone - the capacity of that love is meaningless if it outweighs your capacity to forgive."
*recommended by @walstonreads

"Courage doesn't always roar.
Sometimes courage is the little voice
at the end of the day that says I'll try
again tomorrow."
— Mary Anne Radmacher

*recommended by @bookish_katastrophe

"**But now that I have you, I'm lonely when I'm alone.**"

*recommended by @walstonreads

33

"And as hard as this choice is, we break the pattern before the pattern breaks us."

*recommended by @walstonreads

"It takes courage to grow up and become who you really are."
—E.E. Cummings
*recommended by
@bookandteabook

"Being forgotten, she thinks, is a bit like going mad. You begin to wonder what is real, if you are real. After all, how can a thing be real if it cannot be remembered?"
— V.E. Schwab, The Invisible Life of Addie LaRue

"Throughout the day, I hear this type of thinking from men and women who put all of their energy into just surviving the day, who allow their lack of self-worth to take over and rule every area of their lives."
— Sarah Khalil A.A., Journal Of Life

"He's more myself than I am.
Whatever our souls are made of, his
and mine are the same."
— Emily Brontë, Wuthering Heights

"Be with me always - take any form - drive me mad! only do not leave me in this abyss, where I cannot find you! Oh, God! it is unutterable! I can not live without my life! I can not live without my soul!"
— Emily Brontë, Wuthering Heights

"But someone once told me we always end up where we're meant to be, and this is where I'm meant to be. With you."
— Ana Huang, Twisted Games

"Your memory feels like home to me. So whenever my mind wanders, it always finds it's way back to you."
—Ranata Suzuki

"If you're searching for a quote that puts your feelings into words – you won't find it. You can learn every language and read every word ever written – but you'll never find what's in your heart. How can you? He has it."

— Ranata Suzuki

"Some people are nobody's enemies
but their own, you know."
— Charles Dickens, Oliver Twist

"The world will always choose convenience over reality. It's easier to hate, blame, and fear than it is to understand. No one wants the truth; they want entertainment."

— Chris Colfer, The Wishing Spell

"Being vulnerable doesn't mean you're weak. It means you trust yourself to be strong enough to handle the hurt. It's actually the purest form of strength."
— Lucy Score, Things We Hide from the Light

45

"However, unpopular opinion here. You're not responsible for how you were brought up, but you are responsible for your actions and reactions once you're an adult."

— Lucy Score, Things We Hide from the Light

> "Now that I've forgiven myself, the reminders of him only make me smile."
> — Colleen Hoover, Reminders of Him

"Reading is a hobby, but for some of us, it's an escape from the difficulties we face. To all of you who escape into books, I want to thank you for escaping into this one."
—Colleen Hoover, Reminders of Him

"I never got to fall out of love. I just had to move on."
—Christina Lauren, Love and Other Words

49

"Tell her you love her. Girls need the words."
— Christina Lauren, Love and Other Words

"Allah (swt) reserves the most intense love, care, respect and attachments in our hearts for the person whom He has written for us "

"You say "Tomorrow I'll change" but what if today is your last tomorrow?"

"Can't call this home,
we cry more than we laugh
here.
There has to be another
place."

"Someday ,your sorrows will blossom , a breathtaking spring in your heart"

"Some people are part of the journey but not the destination"

"It takes both rain and sun to
grow beautiful flowers..
It takes both light and dark to
grow a strong you "

"I hope you are blessed with a heart like a wildflower. Strong enough to rise again after being trampled upon, tough enough to weather the worst summer storms, and able to grow and flourish even in the most broken places"

"Keep your dignity and don't be heavy on anyone, for whoever wants you is looking for you even in crowds , and whoever doesn't want you will not see you even if you are infront of him"

"And after every breaking, we realize that destiny has a different opinion, which doesn't resemble our dreams"
— Mahmoud Darwish

"No one is sent by accident to anyone, it's all written"

"Forgive others not because they deserve forgiveness , but because you deserve peace"

"How do I say I miss you in a way that will make your heart aches as mine does?"

— Mahmoud Darwish

"When a thing disturbs the peace of your heart , give it up"

— Prophet Muhammad (pbuh)

"Books are like mirrors: if a fool looks in, you cannot expect a genius to look out."
—J.K. Rowling

"I wish for you to know that you have been the last dream of my soul "

— Charles Dickens

"In a crowded place , our eyes
still met, from a distance ,
each other's voice , we still
heard
What a special
love my heart feels
How can I ever forget?"
— Hashim Y.A.

67

"When love ends, I realize
that it wasn't love .
For love is to be lived not
remembered "
— Mahmoud Darwish

68

"When you realize you've never been put first your whole life, you're just the person who fills a void in people's lives until they don't need you anymore."

"What's the point of having a voice if you're gonna be silent in those moments you shouldn't be?"
— "The Hate U Give" by Angie Thomas

"My grandpa once told me: "You relax on a plan even though , you don't know the pilot. You relax on the ship even though you don't know the captain. Why don't you relax in life , knowing that God is in control..? ."

"I no longer believed in the idea of soul mates, or love at first sight. But I was beginning to believe that a very few times in your life, if you were lucky, you might meet someone who was exactly right for you. Not because he was perfect, or because you were, but because your combined flaws were arranged in a way that allowed two separate beings to hinge together."

— Lisa Kleypas, Blue-Eyed Devil

"Hi Myself,
I know on the outside you may look calm ,laughs ,talks a lot and seems very happy .
Bu deep inside , you're crying and dying because of anger and emotions that you've been holding for too long.
The reason why you keep your feelings , is because you can't explain them"

"I grew up mom. You can not carry me anymore.
My worries are more now ,My list of dreams is taller than me. I grew so much that I can not knock on your door at night and cry"

"She took my black heart with her the day she left, and if she says no, she can keep it. I'm ruined for anyone else anyway."

— Neva Altaj, Painted Scars

"do not look for healing
at the feet of those
who broke you"
— Rupi Kaur, milk and honey

"The world will always choose convenience over reality. It's easier to hate, blame, and fear than it is to understand. No one wants the truth; they want entertainment."
— Chris Colfer, The Wishing Spell

"It is better to be hated for what you are than to be loved for what you are not."
— Autumn Leaves by André Gide

"Sometimes weak and wan, sometimes strong and full of light. The moon understands what it means to be human."
— Shatter Me by Tahereh Mafi

79

"She decided long ago that life was a long journey. She would be strong, and she would be weak, and both would be okay"

— Furthermore by Tahereh Mafi

"There is never a time or place for true love. It happens accidentally, in a heartbeat, in a single flashing, throbbing moment."
—The Truth About Forever by Sarah Dessen

"'Even the darkest night will end and the sun will rise.'"
—Les Misérables by Victor Hugo

"There is nothing sweeter in this sad world than the sound of someone you love calling your name"
— The Tale of Despereaux by Kate DiCamillo

"There is some good in this world, and it's worth fighting for."

— J.R.R. Tolkien, The Two Towers

"It is only with the heart that one can see rightly; what is essential is invisible to the eye."

— Antoine de Saint-Exupéry, The Little Prince

"'Why did you do all this for me?' he asked. 'I don't deserve it. I've never done anything for you.' 'You have been my friend,' replied Charlotte. 'That in itself is a tremendous thing.'"
— E.B. White, Charlotte's Web

"Memories warm you up from the inside. But they also tear you apart."
— Haruki Murakami, Kafka on the Shore

"Who controls the past controls the future. Who controls the present controls the past."
— George Orwell, Nineteen Eighty-Four

"Life is to be lived, not controlled; and humanity is won by continuing to play in face of certain defeat."

— Ralph Ellison, Invisible Man

"There are some things you learn best in calm, and some in storm."

— Willa Cather, The Song of the Lark

"The tongue is like a lion, if you let it loose, it will wound someone."

— Ali ibn Abu Talib

"The world breaks everyone, and afterward, many are strong at the broken places."
— Ernest Hemingway, A Farewell to Arms

"How do you expect Allah to give you the right person , when you are still the wrong person for the right person?"

"When someone shows you who they are believe them the first time."

— Maya Angelou

"And I knew , from the beginning
that I found you to lose you
and loved you to miss you.
Because we met by
coincidence"
— Mahmoud Darwish

"Stab the body and it heals
but injure the heart
and the wound lasts a
lifetime"
— Mineko Iwasaki

"Hearts can break.
Yes, hearts can break,
sometimes I think
it would be better if we died
when they did , but we don't"
— Stephen king

"And maybe what awaits you is better than what you have lost."

"The perfection of Tawheed is found when there remains nothing in the heart except Allah."

— Imam Ibn al-Qayyim

"Whoever mocks his brother for a sin they repented from will not die till he himself falls into the same sin."
— Imam Ibn al-Qayyim

"My sin burdened me heavily. But when I measured it against Your Grace, O Lord, Your forgiveness came out greater."

— Imam Shafi'i

Acknowledgments

First and foremost, I would like to express my deepest gratitude to my parents and siblings for their unwavering support and love. Your encouragement has been a constant source of strength throughout this journey.

I also want to extend my heartfelt thanks to the wonderful individuals who contributed to the creation of this book. Your passion for words and wisdom has been truly inspiring. Special thanks to:

- @mia.read.it
- @moonlitbookmoth
- @bookandteabook
- @bookish_katastrophe
- @every.atom.reads
- @shiros.world
- @mamarachauthor
- @walstonreads

Your insights and shared love for literature have enriched this collection beyond measure. This book would not have been possible without each of you. Thank you for being a part of this journey and for helping to bring "The Wisdom of Words" to life.

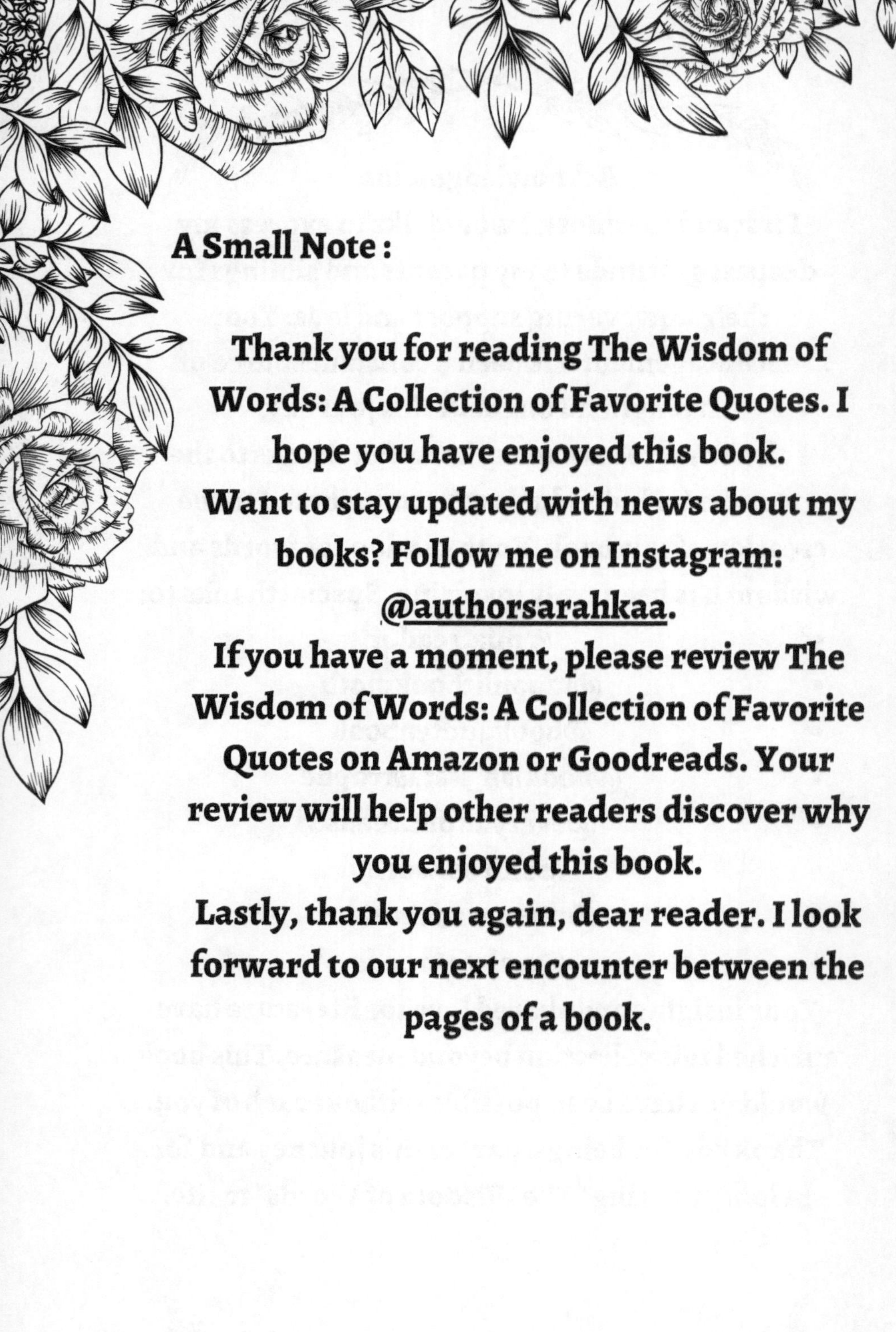

A Small Note :

Thank you for reading The Wisdom of Words: A Collection of Favorite Quotes. I hope you have enjoyed this book.
Want to stay updated with news about my books? Follow me on Instagram: @authorsarahkaa.
If you have a moment, please review The Wisdom of Words: A Collection of Favorite Quotes on Amazon or Goodreads. Your review will help other readers discover why you enjoyed this book.
Lastly, thank you again, dear reader. I look forward to our next encounter between the pages of a book.

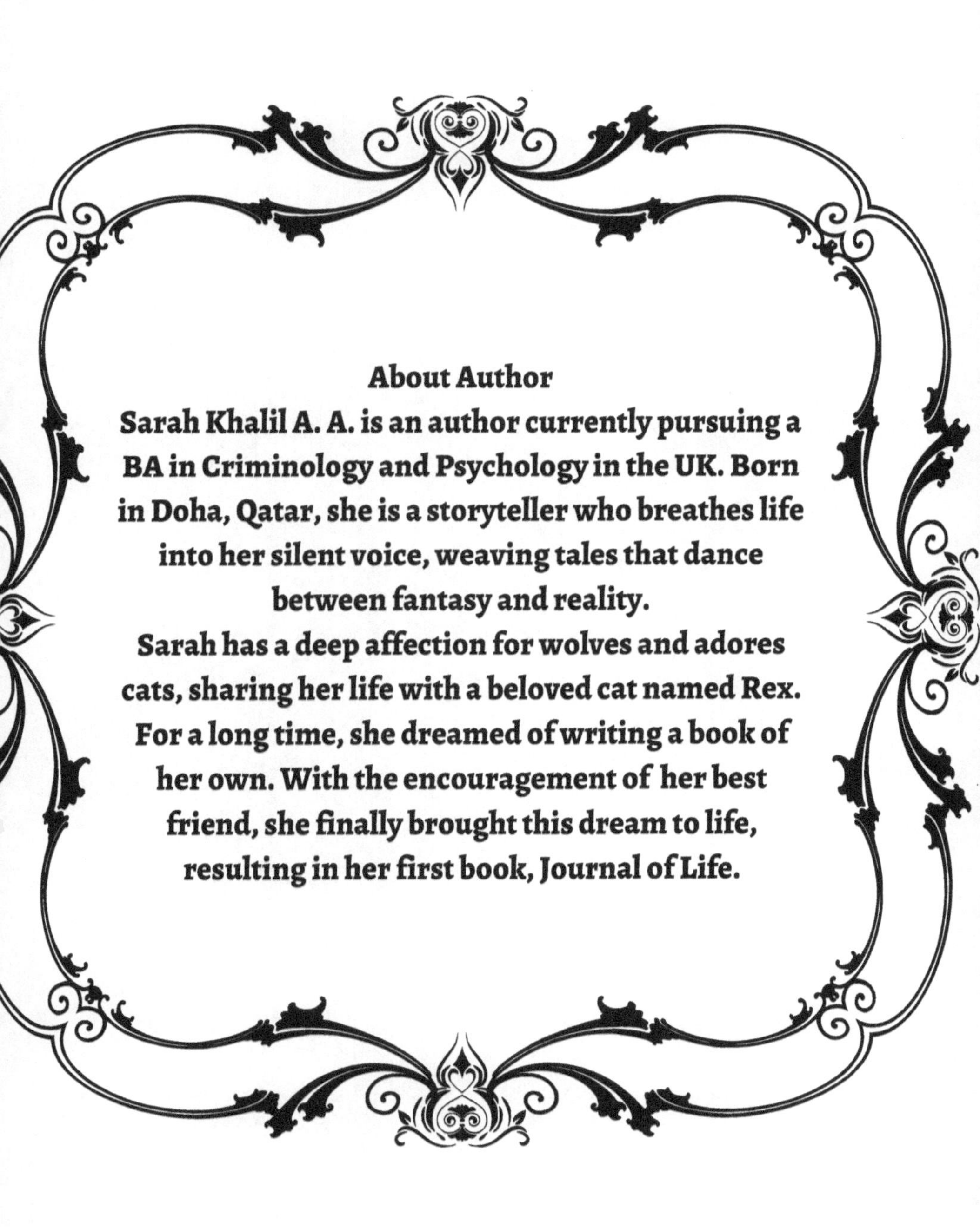

About Author

Sarah Khalil A. A. is an author currently pursuing a BA in Criminology and Psychology in the UK. Born in Doha, Qatar, she is a storyteller who breathes life into her silent voice, weaving tales that dance between fantasy and reality.

Sarah has a deep affection for wolves and adores cats, sharing her life with a beloved cat named Rex. For a long time, she dreamed of writing a book of her own. With the encouragement of her best friend, she finally brought this dream to life, resulting in her first book, Journal of Life.